Proven Strategies
for Business Success

The Role
of Marketing & Advertising
to Grow Your Business

PROVEN STRATEGIES
FOR BUSINESS SUCCESS

THE ROLE
OF MARKETING & ADVERTISING
TO GROW YOUR BUSINESS

OS HILLMAN

ASLAN GROUP
PUBLISHING

Aslan Group Publishing
PO Box 69
Cumming, Georgia 30028 USA
678.455.6262
www.marketplaceleaders.org

ISBN: 978-1888582260

TABLE OF CONTENTS

INTRODUCTION

The world of marketing and advertising has changed dramatically since the dawn of the internet. Google, Facebook, YouTube, Twitter, LinkedIn, smart phones and websites have changed the marketing landscape. Combine this with hundreds of cable TV channels, accessing smart phones and iPads and other hand held devices with mobile apps for programming and information – it's downright mind boggling to the marketer from days past. It has increased the power of relationship marketing exponentially.

A few years ago the movie *Majority Report* with Tom Cruise gave us a glimpse of the future when one scene shows Tom entering a department store and the store windows address him by name and begin to present products unique to his interest. This is our future.

Go on your Facebook page today and you will see products appear on your page that you will have an interest. Marketing experts are targeting you! You couldn't hide if you wanted to today.

Still, there are some proven principles and marketing wisdom that can be applied to these new technologies that do stand the test of time. There may be different delivery tools, but the motivations and strategies to get a response from a customer are still quite similar.

In this ebook I hope to bring some age old marketing and advertising wisdom I have learned over forty years to the exciting world of digital marketing and relationship marketing.

I hope I can provide some insights that will make you a better marketer.

Sincerely,

Os Hillman

1

WHAT BUSINESS
ARE YOU REALLY IN?

One of the first things you have to determine to be successful in your business is to understand what business you're really in. You say, "That's easy, I'm in the computer business." Well, that may or may not be true. You may sell computers, but that may not be the actual business you're in. Apple Computer would probably disagree that computers are your primary business. Your real business, like Apple, is information management. You sell ways to help people manage information better to make life simpler, more productive, and more profitable. That is a whole different concept. Thus, if you try to sell the features of your computers over the benefits, you are likely to fail at effectively selling your product.

Recently, I attended a conference in Naples, Florida, held at the Ritz-Carlton Hotel. What struck me about the hotel is that they really aren't in the hotel business—they are in the service business. The reason you pay top price for staying at the Ritz-Carlton is for the service and amenities they offer. And few hotels do it better than the Ritz-Carlton. From the time you walk on the property until the time you leave, you know the number one priority of the people who work there is to provide outstanding service to the guest. It is ingrained in every detail—from the maid service personnel to management.

American Express is another company you might incorrectly assume is in the financial service business. Actually, American Express is in the image and convenience business. Think about it. American Express has worked hard to convey that you are "somebody" if you use an American Express Card™ instead of a Visa or MasterCard. They are selling "image." They are selling convenience. From hundreds of thousands of establishments who accept the card, to automated teller machines worldwide, to buyer protection plans, American Express is dedicated to positioning itself as the card that provides the most services, especially for the business market. AmEx cards account for approximately 24% of the total dollar volume of credit card transactions in the US. In 1975, David Ogilvy of Ogilvy & Mather developed the highly successful Don't Leave Home Without Them ad campaign for American Express Travelers Cheques, featuring Oscar-award-winning actor Karl Malden. Karl Malden served as the public face of American Express Travelers Cheques for 25 years. Only in recent years have other cards become competitive. Even so, among higher income professionals American Express remains at the top.

What business are you in? Have you really thought about it? It may make a big difference in how you market yourself and your services.

Sandi Krakowski, a top rated social media expert in the world says every marketer should start with an idea and then ask yourself these questions:

- What is the desired result of this product/service?

- What is the customer already saying they want/need from this product/service?

- How does your result and process differ from everyone else?

- How is it being done by others and what do customers say?

2

POSITIONING:
YOU, YOUR PRODUCT, YOUR COMPANY

For the last decade, the word positioning has gotten a lot of attention in the advertising world. Gone are the days when advertising simply promoted the benefits of the product or service on merit alone to attract the broad audience. Nowadays that won't work. Our media crazed society is too big for a product to be sold in this manner.

Before I explain why this is true, let's back up for a moment and define positioning. I have heard many different definitions. The one that makes best sense to me is the place or product, service, company, person or any other thing occupies in the mind of the one viewing it. Simply stated, positioning is the personality. It identifies what the product does and who it is for. Positioning is used to create a niche in the market you can command. The premise being that by narrowing your focus to a realistic target market, you are better able to deliver your message and capture that market. You position the product in the mind of the prospect.

What's Your Position?

Did you know that you have a position in the minds of those who know you? You may be known as the peacemaker or the computer nerd or Mr. Fix-It. People may come to you because of the position you own among them.

Products that have definite positions are bought because of the position they retain. Dove soap could have been positioned as a detergent bar for men with dirty hands, but David Ogilvy chose instead to position it as a cosmetic bar for women with dry skin—a position it still holds after 40 years. Crest Toothpaste could have been positioned as a breath freshener or whitener; instead it has been positioned as a cavity fighter year after year. What position does Walmart hold? Answer: Low price leader. How about Cadillac? Answer: High end, older, wealthy demographic profile. Positioning is identifying the product with a personality. And it is the single most important element in selling a product or service beyond the product itself.

Developing A Positioning Statement

Companies need proper positioning in order to effectively market themselves. Developing a positioning statement is the first step. Consider the positioning statement adopted by many of the more visible companies: Panasonic—*Just Slightly Ahead Of Our Time*; GE—*We Bring Good Things To Life*; Xerox—*Our Quality Can't Be Duplicated*; Mercedes—*Engineered Like No Other Car In The World*. Notice how each of the statements say something about what they are best known for, but in a way that is simple, and often with a double meaning. Let's examine some case studies, and how these successful companies demonstrated positioning in creative and practical ways.

Software for the Large Law Firm

A computer company wanted to appeal to large law firms for their hardware and software business. Large law firms are usually managed by a legal administrator. The computer company's basic selling position was that they had a good product and had exceptional service to back it up. Here are some ways we established their position in practical advertising strategies:

1. By using a model who represented a law firm administrator we targeted the group we wanted most to reach.

2. By visually representing several lawyers in the ad and making reference to an actual number, we qualified the size of the firm we wanted to appeal to.

3. And by developing a headline and visual that represented the main character, the legal administrator, we were able to empathize with our target audience.

Positioning a Restaurant

How would a restaurant go about positioning itself if it wanted to attract young urban professionals? Let's look at how to position a restaurant like this for success.

1. Develop a menu that caters to the clientele.

2. Create a décor that attracts your target group: Stylish furniture, stained glass windows, contemporary styling.

3. Create slice of life advertising showing the type of people you want to visit your restaurant. These people are doing the same things your clientele like to do…sailing, playing golf, etc.

4. Place your advertising in appropriate media where these people can read, hear, or see your message.

Add all of this up and you've created a positioning strategy to reach the urban professional.

A Community Bank

Finally, let's see how a small town community bank might approach their positioning problem. The bank wants to create an image of a small, hometown bank that prides itself in service and friendliness. Here are some strategies we might want to incorporate.

1. Train your tellers to address each customer by name. Learn the regular customers so you know them by name each time they come into the bank.

2. Use advertising that focuses on your people. Their friendliness, their smiles, their service commitment.

3. Be the biggest sponsor of community projects to insure that the bank is perceived as a supporter or local activities that benefit the community as a whole.

4. Create a service award that is given annually to the individual who makes the most contributions to you community. (By the bank's connecting with this award the bank benefits by mere association with such an honorable endeavor.)

What About Me?

So how does this relate to you? Think about you, your product, and your company. Have you defined your position clearly in your own mind? If not, ask those around you. Conduct some market research to see how the market perceives your product or service. You might be surprised. If you can start with a strongly held perception, it will be much easier to establish a position than to create one from scratch.

THE CONTENTS OF A PLAN: WHAT'S IN, WHAT'S OUT

The purpose of a marketing plan is to simplify the execution of the marketing idea: moving goods or services from concept to customer. You may ask, "Why do I even need a plan?" The answer is because without it, you are likely to use your limited resources in a wasteful way and thereby fail in the effort. For almost everything we do, we have a plan to accomplish it.

Whether your plan is one page, five pages, or fifty pages, a good plan will always have the basic SOS formula:

Situation—Where are we now?

Objective—Where are we going?

Strategy—How are we going to get there?

These elements do not always have to be in this order, but any good marketing plan will have this formula included.

Before starting your plan, the first step is to write an outline. You may not need every topic, but using this outline as a check list will determine if it applies to your situation. The following outline represents all the basic ingredients of a good marketing plan:

I. Corporate Objective
II. Situation Analysis
  A. Market Current Situation
  B. Direct Competition
    1. Market Share
    2. Position
    3. Creative
    4. Spending
  C. Indirect Competition
  D. Target Audience
    1. Demographics
    2. Psychographics
    3. Trends
    4. Problems & Opportunities
III. Marketing Objectives
IV. Strategies
  A. Positioning Product
  B. Price
  C. Packaging
  D. Distribution
  E. Promotion
  F. Creative
  G. Media
  H. Direct Mail Tactics
  I. Budget
V. Projections

Now that you have your basic outline, let's discuss what each topic entails.

Corporate Objective: Before you can devise an effective plan, know where the chief executive officer is taking the company. Where does he/she want to be in two years? Five years? Or even ten years? If you don't know this, you are going to spend a lot of wasted time and energy developing a plan that may be totally opposed to the philosophy of the company. Sit down with the CEO and find out this information. Then, condense it into one or two sentences. You now have the Corporate Objective for the company.

Situation Analysis: Here's where the 90% of the work lies. Conducting a Situation Analysis is where market research occurs. Research can be an invaluable tool to help determine the necessary strategies to take in your marketing plan. However, research alone is insufficient. It needs to be objectively reviewed. An example is Coca-Cola's use of market research in the decision to introduce New Coke. Research indicated that consumers liked the taste of New Coke. Unfortunately, their research didn't convey the tremendous emotional attachment consumers had to the old product. The result was almost devastating.

Market/Current Situation: Describe the market in which you are competing. How large is the market? How many players are in the market? How do you fit within this market? You may need professional market research, or conduct some of your own with what I call "bird dog" research. Find out as much as you can about the product and companies in the marketplace. Paint a picture of how your company fits into this overall market.

Direct Competition: Who are your direct competitors? If you can, state the sales and size of each one of these competitors. See where you fit into the scheme of things.

Share: What is your current market share? If you do not have a product in the market, find out who owns what share of the marketplace among your competitors.

Position: How is your company perceived in the marketplace? Notice I didn't say how do you think you are perceived. Only an outsider can tell you how you are truly perceived. This is best done through research. How is your company positioned in the marketplace? And how is your competition positioned? Are you known for your quality of service? Research will uncover the unique traits of your product or service? Eventually any negative trait—from poor service, to slow delivery—will have a negative impact on your business.

Creative: How does your competition portray their creative product? Is their advertising effective? What is the value of their packaging? Examine every area of the physical nature of your competition.

Spending: How much is being spent by your competitor? How does that compare to your company? Your competitor may be spending more in packaging or perhaps investing more to reach the trade market, or they may even be spending more in direct mail. Find out what their emphasis is and where most of their advertising dollars are invested.

Indirect Competition: Sometimes it is important to look beyond the direct competition and to focus on indirect competition. A good example of indirect competition for a book store might be records and gifts found in a competitor's bookstore. Is the direct competition other books, or is it in fact the records and gifts that are also found in a competitor's bookstore?

Target Audience: Who do you really want to sell this product to? Who is the prime audience for this product? You'll want to break this down in terms of demographics and psychographics by asking questions like: How old is the target audience? Are they middle class? College educated? Paint a profile of the individual most likely to buy this product. This is going to be especially important when you start planning your media buys.

Trends: What are the current trends that relate to your product? Has it been a down economy for this product or are forecasters predicting a bright future? Take a look at the industry in terms of the past, the present, and the future.

Problems and Opportunities: By now you have had the opportunity to identify problems. You will be able to recognize your weaknesses and your strengths as they compare to your competitor's. A good marketing plan turns a problem into an opportunity. This can work for your product, too. The problems you've worked so hard to unearth can become opportunities. Try to draw concrete conclusions from your problems and opportunities. These will be important to you in establishing your marketing objectives and strategies.

Marketing Objectives: Here's where you want to state in clear, simple and achievable terms what your Marketing Objective is. Be specific. Increasing sales is not a Marketing Objective. Increasing sales by 4% in 2016 is a Marketing Objective. Declare that you will achieve your Marketing Objective! Now you are going to show how you will do it. However, perhaps you have gotten to this point and discovered through your research that it is impossible to achieve a 4% increase in sales based on your findings. If you sincerely believe this, then it is your responsibility to state it unapologetically. Be realistic in your projections and make your projections based on the facts you have.

Strategies: Our Strategies section tells what action is needed to achieve your marketing objective.

Product Positioning: How do you want to position your product? If your product is toothpaste do you want it to be positioned as a "whitener" or a "breath freshener"?

Price: How do you want to market the product? Above market, below market, or in-between?

Package: How do you want to package this product? Will it have four-color? Will is be packaged similarly to your competitor's product? Perhaps you will do something totally different in the packaging area. One of the greatest examples of the impact of packaging on a product is in the pantyhose industry. For years pantyhose was packaged in flat boxes and mostly marketed through department stores. Now through the efforts of L'eggs, women can go to quick-stops and other outlets to buy pantyhose found in unique egg-shaped packaging.

Distribution: Do you want to change the way the customer can get the product? If it is a book, do you want him to find it in a specialty bookstore? Or can you reach the customer through a grocery store or other outlet?

Promotion: Do you want to use contests, sweepstakes, or give-aways in your strategies of selling the product?

Creative: How do you creatively present your product to the market-place? Will you use humor, "slice-of-life" approaches, or product-oriented advertising?

Media: What forms of media will best reach your targeted customer? Is this product best suited for television, radio, print, direct mail, email, online, social media, Google ads, etc?

Promotion: What other avenues can you pursue to promote this product? Perhaps you need to do a full PR campaign on the release of the product.

Budget/Projections: Here's where you state what it is going to cost in order to accomplish your objective. Not only will you produce a budget, but also want to project sales based on that budget. The plan does not necessarily have to show profit on the product during the first year. Proctor & Gamble states it takes 18-24 months before they get on the upswing of any new product. But, remember, it must make a profit at some point!

A good marketing plan will be an invaluable tool for your organization. It is your track to run on. A detailed, concise plan takes the guesswork out of the marketing process and insures you the greatest opportunity for a successful marketing effort.

CHAPTER

4

DOES ADVERTISING
REALLY WORK?

A friend of mine once said to me, "You know, I really don't think advertising works. I mean, I've never bought a product because I've seen or heard some advertisement." His statement caused much consternation on my part, as I was in the ad agency business at the time and knew this simply was a false statement that I could prove.

I posed the following situation to him: What if you had to drive to your local grocery store to pick up a can of tomato sauce, and you had never bought this product before. Suppose you are not familiar with the brand names. So you will probably make your choice of product when you get to the aisle of the store. When you leave the store you turn the radio on as you're driving. You hear an ad talking about Maria's Sauce. You turn the corner and there is a billboard advertising Maria's Sauce. You have to stop for gas on the way and pick up a magazine. You look through the magazine as you're waiting to pay for your gas, and there is an ad for Maria's sauce. Finally, you get to the store and at the front of the store there are coupons available for all sorts of products. Yes, a coupon for Maria's Sauce is there.

You are now in the aisle of the store and you are looking at all the brands of tomato sauce. You don't know which sauce to buy. But for the last 20 minutes you have seen all the ads for Maria's Sauce. You have probably not even noticed the ads but you do recall seeing Maria's somewhere.

Your subconscious remembers and YOU BUY MARIA'S SAUCE. This illustration may seem far fetched to some. But that is exactly how advertising works. Years ago a friend once said, "Advertising is like a piece of pie. You never know which slice is going to sell your product, but the whole pie is important to the selling of the product." Which slice of the pie sold Maria's Sauce? That would pretty hard to determine. But we can be sure the sale would not have been made without all the advertising that led up to the point of decision.

Advertising does affect a number of factors in the selling process. Cahners Publishing Company in Massachusetts has done a number of studies on the effects of advertising among businesses. The research has clearly shown advertising is not a frill activity; but rather is a necessary and important part of a business' marketing operations.

The studies also found that it isn't enough that a product is advertised: of even greater importance is the amount of advertising. The businesses that advertise more than their competitors get better results. To a large extent the study found that a product image is as it relates to quality is determined by the way and degree of advertising. And, quality is the single most important factor in making a sale.

Much of advertising is an art as well as a science. A lot is known about the way it works, how it interacts with other aspects of the marketing operations of a business, and the way it helps to build profitability. Of course, advertising alone cannot make a business profitable. But it is a crucial element in a successful business.

Many years ago, a well-known advertising executive was asked to define advertising. His reply, "Advertising is salesmanship in print." (At the time this statement was made, there were no television or radio ads.)

How important is advertising to the actual selling of a product? Rosser Reeves, the advertising genius of the 1940s states, "Advertising is only one of 37 factors which affects the sale of a product or service." Other factors include quality, service, price, seasonality, distribution, audience, economy, and position.

As the president of Proctor and Gamble once stated so honestly, "We spend millions of dollars on advertising but cannot accurately say whether the return on our advertising dollar is justified or not. All we know is that if we don't advertise, we pay the penalty of poor sales."

This becomes even more remarkable when you know how many dollars are spent on research to determine the effectiveness of advertising. Large advertising firms spend millions of dollars a year conducting market research to insure the successful sale of a product. And many times, if a campaign is not a success, the agency gets the blame. Is it any wonder there are so many failures by small companies who don't conduct research feel it is an unnecessary expense and would rather take the risk?

Net sales seem to be the determining factor in ascertaining whether or not a company's advertising is successful. However, this is not always the case. Sometimes uncontrollable factors do arise.

When Coca-Cola introduced New Coke, a great deal of market research was done on the new product and a strategy for introducing it. Tests proved that consumers liked the taste. Advertising was created and tested. Everything pointed in the right direction. You know the rest of the story.

Coke consumers created a national furor. The emotional trauma of loyal Coke drinkers had never been considered. There was a perception in the consumers' minds that part of their lives had been taken away—and no one had even asked their opinion. It was, in their minds, like changing the color of the American flag. You don't change something so intrinsic in the lives of the customers without reaping the consequences. Coke did.

We could cite hundreds of other factors that affect the sales of a product. What if the product is inferior to others on the market? What if the price is too high? What if the economy drops out right at the beginning of the campaign? Or, what if your product or company receives some bad publicity? The greatest advertising in the world won't sell a product under these circumstances.

All 37 factors must be in place if a product is to have a chance for success. A good product, a competitive price, proper positioning, a knowledge and understanding of the buyer, a large enough market, a sales and distribution network, and effective advertising are all pieces of the puzzle that add up to a successful business.

GENERATING LEADS: ACQUIRING A NEW CUSTOMER

Once we've successfully positioned our product or service, we are ready to pursue prospective customers. Some of our best sources of new business come from our existing customer base. We can reach these customers in a number of ways. One of these is through the publication of an ongoing newsletter or blog which allows our customers to get to know us, or our product and service in a more relaxed manner. Having faithful customers is great, but it is absolutely essential that a small business be continually developing new business by attracting and acquiring new prospects. In the direct-mail industry we call this lead-generation. Lead-generation takes place when a point of contact is made between a potential customer and you. This can be done in a number of ways:

Seminars, Special Events, Trade Shows

Participation in these types of events provides public exposure, a means to distribute brochures, and opportunity to meet potential customers.

Effective Use of Premiums

If you decide to use a premium in the marketing program, keep in mind what the premium should be able to accomplish. First, the purpose of the premium is to motivate someone to contact you who would not normally not contact you without the use of a premium. Probably the most popular and over-used premium the resort real-estate industry uses is offering the customer a free weekend in return for viewing their property. The logic behind this strategy says that real estate companies feel so confident in their ability to sell property to the prospect, that they are willing to offer a free two night stay at the property for the opportunity to make their sales presentation.

Another type of premium is a booklet or free eBook or podcast on a related service that would be valuable to the prospect. The value of this type of promotion is that it gives the potential audience a taste of your knowledge in your particular in industry. It provides the potential customer with something of value and creates a means of contact between you and your potential audience without the need for personal contact. Usually a response link at the end of the ebook or call to action web address allows the prospect to make further contact by actually making a purchase or requesting more information. We used this approach in a recent promotion to prospects for a carpet manufacturer. A free carpet care brochure was offered to potential customers by simply responding to the direct-mail offer. Now days online marketing is more likely to offer digital products like ebooks or a podcast or video presentation.

Premium marketing can be applied to virtually every type of industry. For instance, the insurance professional might ask for a booklet on Ten Things To Remember The Next Time You Buy Life Insurance. One investment group offered to an ebooklet entitled Your 15-Minute Retirement Plan. Investment managers often offer a fee dinner in return for your time to view their presentation. A software company might want to offer a free 30-day trial on his particular product that gives the potential customer the opportunity to try the product before he actually buys it. The goal of all of these approaches is to create a point of contact between you and a potential new customer that did not exist before. The purpose for creating an ongoing lead generation program is keep a pipeline of potential new customers coming your way. This will help eliminate the peaks and valleys that are so common to small businesses.

There are many ways to build a mailing list. If you already have a mailing list you could offer to swap emailing with another organization that might have a similar profile as yours. This cost each of your organization nothing, but has a potential big upside. You send your offer to your list, they send your offer to their list.

6

HOW MUCH SHOULD YOU SPEND ON ADVERTISING?

Determining how much to spend on advertising for a product or service can be difficult. There are three primary methods commonly accepted among marketers on evaluating how much to spend.

Know What You Want To Accomplish

If you want to release a new product to the market and want to capture a 75 percent market share for this category, you may need to have a 15-20 percent of projected sales and budget in order to accomplish your goal. On the other hand, you may have a consistent ten percent share of the market and want to maintain what you have with no new entries into the marketplace. In this case, you may have a three percent ad-to-sales ratio expense.

Know What Your Competition Is Doing

If you want to stay competitive with your competition you will need to spend at least the same amount as they did. If you want to be aggressive in gaining new market share, you will want to increase your ad spending.

Determine A Percentage Of Sales

A percentage of sales is the most common way to determine what should be spent on advertising. However, this may not necessarily be the best factor in committing your advertising dollars. Every business is different and espouses different business objectives. Your business may market primarily through a certain type of distribution system, whereas another may have an altogether different mode of distribution, with each system having particular expenses. For instance, one year Ad Age cited jewelry manufacturers as spending 18.8 percent of sales for advertising compared to book publishers spending 3.1 percent. Every industry varies in advertising expense-to-sales ratios because sales vary by industry even for individual products and services within an industry.

When assigning budgetary amounts for advertising the first place to start is to determine what others are spending in your industry. Secondly, determine what your goals are. Study your competition to see what they are doing and plan accordingly. And lastly, evaluate your method of distribution. A company that sells all their products through mail order catalogs is going to have a much larger advertising expense than a company selling through commissioned sales reps.

Survey of Advertising-To-Sales Ratios By Industry	% Of Sales
Air Transportation	2.0
Books: Publishing & Printing	3.1
Cigarettes	4.2
Computers & Software Warehouses	10.5
Department Stores	2.5
Miscellaneous Manufacturing Industries	4.4
Furniture Stores	7.1
Jewelry & Watches Warehouses	18.8
Retail Stores	7.0
Sporting & Athletic Goods	5.2

Source: AdAge

SHOULD YOU ADVERTISE
IN A WEAK ECONOMY?

Often during an economic downturn companies will ask if advertising should be curtailed. Some don't even raise the question, it's just the first thing they cut. Companies who do this may view advertising as a luxury and not a necessity for maintaining growth during slow economic periods.

But what are the facts?

During the recession years of 1974-1975, American Business Press studies summarized research that showed the sales and net profit performance of 133 companies. The data shows that companies who did not cut advertising fared much better during and after the recession than those who did. The evidence strongly suggests a cause-and-effect relationship: companies that reduce advertising in periods of economic distress lose ground to their more forward-looking competitors. But the study does not attempt to explain that relationship or investigate its dynamics.

Another study conducted by McGraw-Hill showed that, in the 1974-75 recession, industrial companies which maintained or increased advertising experienced higher sales growth during the recession. By 1978, three years after the recession, sales of companies which were aggressive advertisers held a 53 percent margin of leadership over the companies which cut or eliminated advertising.

The Association of Business Publishers hired the research firm of Meldrum and Fewsmith and found conclusively that advertising during recessions not only increases sales but also boosts profits. This has held true for all U.S. post-World War II recessions (1954, 1958, 1961, 1970, 1975-75, and 1981-82.)

Companies who continue to invest in advertising during slow economic periods have the opportunity to gain market share by staying aggressive while others cut back. Those companies who have managed well and are financially sound will fare better during slow economic times compared to their competition.

Companies may not be able to keep the sales level they enjoyed during a good economy, but compared to competitors who cut back on advertising, they will fare better.

Imagine that you are the captain of a ship sailing across the Atlantic and you encounter strong winds that threaten to drive your ship backward. You have to be in the harbor by a certain date. First, you would drop your sails and tighten up your ship to withstand the onslaught on the storm. But your engines would remain full throttle in an effort to move toward your destination. Conversely, if you were to simply cut off all engines, you would be at the mercy of the winds. This would cause the ship to go miles off course, resulting in a much greater loss of time and possible peril.

A business is much the same. All businesses encounter rough seas from time to time. Businesses that cut back their advertising lose ground to more aggressive, better managed companies. They will seize the opportunity to attract your customers and maintain their steady, albeit slower growth during a lean economy.

When faced with budget cuts in your business due to a slow economy, think twice before slashing your advertising. You might just be cutting your company's lifeline to future success and putting your company at the mercy of the economic winds.

8

BUSINESS-TO-BUSINESS ADVERTISING

Business-to-business direct marketing is simply one business marketing directly to another. This may come through all forms of marketing and advertising. Before you start a marketing program for your business, ask yourself some questions: How much can I afford to spend to get a lead? How much is a customer worth to our organization? Without knowing the answers to these two questions, your marketing strategies will be ineffective and possibly very costly.

Cost per lead and cost per sale are common terms used in the direct-marketing industry. They fall just behind the three most important words in direct marketing-list, list, and list! How much is a sale worth to your company? $10, $100, $1,000, $10,000, $100,000? The answer to this question will significantly determine your marketing strategies to attract a lead and then convert that lead to a sale. Let me cite an example:

A software company determined that if they were able to get a prospect to view their software through a product demonstration, the conversion-to-sale ratio percentage was quite high. A software and hardware sale in their product category could result in a sale of $50,000 to $150,000 depending on the size of the prospect's company. With this information, we developed an aggressive direct mail program incorporating an attractive premium for any prospect who responded by reserving a demonstration at the once-a-year trade show. This strategy was developed on the premise of two facts:

1. a high close ratio for those who see a demo, and

2. a customer was worth a great deal to our client, both in terms of initial dollars from the sale and in recurring income.

Knowing the value of a customer is important in determining your strategy for getting and keeping the customer. Obviously, if you must make a lot of sales with a lot of different prospects with small profit margins, your strategy must be completely different. Before you begin a direct marketing or online program ask yourself some important questions about your previous twelve months:

- How much did I spend to achieve the sales for the past twelve months (cost of sales)? To get your cost per sale divide the total cost of sales, advertising, and promotion by the number of sales.

- How valuable is my customer? Is he a one-time sale or can he contribute to sales on an ongoing basis? What is the customer's potential contribution?

Plan your marketing budget based on this information.

Taking these factors into account, you can quickly determine if the appropriate budget has been assigned toward acquiring new customers.

CHAPTER

9

NICHE MARKETING: NARROWING YOUR MARKET COULD EXPAND YOUR BUSINESS

Today's successful businesses are requiring more focus on specific marketing for their services and products. Smart companies are realizing that it is becoming increasingly difficult to be everything to everybody. Consequently, niche marketing is becoming more commonplace today. What is niche marketing? Simply put, it is the carving out of a particular market within a market to expand your business. Here are a few examples of what I mean:

Domino's Pizza captured a specialized niche in the market by focusing all their attention on home delivery.

A woman in California started an exercise studio catering to the large woman. Women At Large became a successful franchise because they focused on one particular niche in the exercise market.

A printing company in North Carolina found they could be more effective in selling more printing by specializing in the golf scorecard business instead of becoming known as a general printer. This allowed them to attract business within the golf market.

A software company located in Atlanta, Georgia, was a developer of application software systems for medium-sized businesses for the IBM minicomputers. Today, this company has focused all their attention on developing software and hardware applications for law firms from 30 to 300 in size. This special focus allows them to attract a much more targeted audience and allows them to market to a more defined audience.

In the mid-nineties I began to transition from a career in advertising to a non-profit ministry calling to serve men and women in the workplace. I began teaching about integrating faith into our work life. A few years later I began to be recognized as a leader in the faith at work movement. This became a niche that I am still identified with today.

There are a lot of good reasons to develop a niche within a particular market. Service businesses are especially wise to focus their attention on niche markets because of the referral business they can claim.

For instance, a law firm will often specialize in a few primary areas, as will an accounting firm or architectural firm. But, this is not limited to service businesses only, as exemplified by the case studies mentioned.

By developing a particular niche, you may be able to expand your business in a much greater way than if you had an everything for everybody strategy. The way to do this is to look at your customer base to see if there are any services or products that seem to fit within one particular segment. You may have a series of products that appeal to a certain audience that you may want to package together and promote as a group to that audience.

Examining your own customer base is the first step to determining where niches can be developed. Companies who have established target niches will be the companies who are around in the years to come.

10

THE ARTT PRINCIPLE: DEVELOPING NEW RELATIONSHIPS THAT LEAD TO CUSTOMERS

There is a four-step process I have found very helpful in developing new customers or new donors for my own non-profit. I call it ARTT:

Acquaintance

Relationship

Trust

Transaction

Acquaintance

When beginning a relationship with a customer or ministry partner, it often starts with some sort of handshake. This "handshake", so to speak, is how the person gets to know about your organization. It could be through an event, another person, social media, or a website. This is the beginning of the relationship between you and the potential customer or ministry partner.

Relationship

A relationship between your organization and the person develops when they sign up for something you have. Perhaps it is a free coaching program, a free devotional, or they have liked your Facebook page. Some sort of action has been taken where this person has given you the permission to interact with them. This is the second step in the ARTT process.

Trust

Trust between you and the potential customer or ministry partner develops. They begin to see the results of your product, or the impact your ministry is having on their life and the lives of others. They see credibility, and they begin to trust your organization.

Transaction

A transaction occurs when the potential customer becomes a customer or ministry financial partner. Once the relationship and trust has been developed, they are ready to get what you have to offer, whether it is buying a product, or going to an event or engaging your services.

It is helpful to note that rarely does someone go from acquaintance to transaction without the other first two steps. If it does happen, it is because relationship and trust has been developed already. Permission is a key aspect of both relationship and trust - you must have the person's permission to begin an interaction with them.

Often the best source of increased sales is through your existing customer base. Creating a referral program for your customer to refer others to you can be a very successful strategy.

11

HOW MUCH IS A CUSTOMER WORTH TO YOU?

Customer Lifetime Value is a term with which catalog direct marketers are well acquainted. But retailers and other general marketers find the term foreign to them and have failed to understand the real potential value of a first time buyer.

Purpose

The purpose of the customer lifetime value is to assess the financial value of each customer. Some customers are more equal than others. Customer lifetime value (CLV) differs from customer profitability or CP (the difference between the revenues and the costs associated with the customer relationship during a specified period) in that CP measures the past and Customer Lifetime Value looks forward. As such, CLV can be more useful in shaping managers' decisions but is much more difficult to quantify. While quantifying CP is a matter of carefully reporting and summarizing the results of past activity, quantifying CLV involves forecasting future activity.[2]

Customer lifetime value (CLV)

Customer Lifetime Value is the present value of the future cash flows attributed to the customer during his/her entire relationship with the company.

Present value is the discounted sum of future cash flows: each future cash flow is multiplied by a carefully selected number less than one, before being added together. The multiplication factor accounts for the way the value of money is discounted over time. The time-based value of money captures the intuition that everyone would prefer to get paid sooner rather than later but would prefer to pay later rather than sooner. The multiplication factors depend on the discount rate chosen (10% per year as an example) and the length of time before each cash flow occurs.

For example, money received ten years from now must be discounted more than dollars received five years in the future.[2] CLV applies the concept of present value to cash flows attributed to the customer relationship. Because the present value of any stream of future cash flows is designed to measure the single lump sum value today of the future stream of cash flows, CLV will represent the single lump sum value today of the customer relationship. Even more simply, CLV is the dollar value of the customer relationship to the firm. It is an upper limit on what the firm would be willing to pay to acquire the customer relationship as well as an upper limit on the amount the firm would be willing to pay to avoid losing the customer relationship. If we view a customer relationship as an asset of the firm, CLV would present the dollar value of that asset.[2]

One of the major uses of CLV is customer segmentation, which starts with the understanding that not all customers are equally important. CLV-based segmentation model allows the company to predict the most profitable group of customers, understand those customers' common characteristics, and focus more on them rather than on less profitable customers. CLV-based segmentation can be combined with a Share of Wallet (SOW) model to identify "high CLV but low SOW" customers with the assumption that the company's profit could be maximized by investing marketing resources in those customers.

Customer Lifetime Value metrics are used mainly in relationship-focused businesses, especially those with customer contracts. Examples include banking and insurance services, telecommunications and most of the business-to-business sector. However, the CLV principles may be extended to transactions-focused categories such as consumer packaged goods by incorporating stochastic purchase models of individual or aggregate behavior.

When John Martin came into the local sports athletic store to purchase a warm up suit for $30.00, John became a first-time customer. But what is the value of John as a customer and how much could that store invest to get John to make the first purchase? When John comes into the store, the manager should not see $39.00 as his value to this store, but rather he should see $1,950.00.

$39 sale/year × 10 years × 5 referrals = $1,950.00

Mail order catalogers understand lifetime value and are willing to lose money over a 12-month period when mailing to prospective mailing lists to gain a first-time customer. Once a customer is gained, a major effort is made to turn the first time buyer into a "multi" or a repeat customer. Research has found that if a customer buys more than once, you've got a good chance of keeping that customer over a long period of time.

12

SWEEPSTAKES: YOU MAY ALREADY BE THE WINNER OF $1,000,000!

How many times have you received an envelope in January with a message above in it? Today the Sweepstakes has largely been replaced by the lottery.

Why are lotteries or sweepstakes so popular? Simple. They appeal to our base desire to receive something free or for very little investment of our time. We all would love to hit the jackpot. Let's talk briefly about sweepstakes which is different than a lottery and whether it could be used in your business to increase your sales.

Direct marketers use sweepstakes for one reason only: to increase response. They have been the most successful method of increasing response to a mail offer or online promotion to date. Tests have been conducted over many years for offers for everything from magazine subscriptions to real estate offers to credit card purchases. The average direct mail response can range from 1 to 3%. When a sweepstakes is included in the package, that response could increase 40-60%. Why? Well, how can anyone resist not opening an envelope that says, "You may already be the winner of $1,000,000!" The power of something for nothing is a strong motivator. The first thing direct response marketers teach us is that we must get the prospect to open the envelope or email and once that is accomplished many people will read the rest of the contents.

Contrary to what many believe, one does not have to buy anything to enter the sweepstakes, and federal legislation requires all prizes be awarded. The psychology behind sweepstakes is that it serves to get prospects involved in the package. The more complicated the package, the better.

Direct marketers also make lots of money selling your name after you respond. Even if you don't buy, your name is valuable because you have proven to be a mail responsive person. More and more sensitivity is growing regarding what information people are willing to give online.

How can a sweepstakes help your business? You do not have to have a lot of money to have your own sweepstakes or contest. For a carpet client we recommended a $5,000 Carpet Sweepstakes that went to customers who had purchased carpet within the last twelve months. We wanted to find out more information about our customers and get referrals of friends we could mail to. If we attempted to simply mail a brochure to these people we probably would have gotten a typical 2-3% response. But by adding the sweepstakes option we achieved an incredible 30% response! Our gift award had high perceived value even though the client paid the manufacturing cost which was considerably lower than the list price.

So the next time you have a promotion, why not consider incorporating a sweepstakes? You'll be surprised at the additional response you can generate.

13

HOW TO EVALUATE THE EFFECTIVENESS OF YOUR DIRECT RESPONSE PROMOTION

One of the big differences between general advertising (also known as awareness advertising) and direct response advertising is the method by which advertising effectiveness is determined. For the most part, general advertising has little means of determining immediate success or failure. The final results may not be known for weeks, months, or even years. General advertising campaigns can often be very creative and may even win awards. But there have been many award winning ad campaigns that did nothing to generate sales. One such promotion was the Joe Isuzu television campaign several years ago. It won many industry awards but the sales of Isuzu cars actually went down.

This is the difference between direct response advertising versus general advertising. Direct response advertising is any advertising designed to generate a response via a phone call, online ad, email, video, social media, or direct contact.

Unlike general advertising, direct marketing effectiveness is determined by several measurements. Cost per lead, cost per click, email open rates or cost per order are the most common response factors. Cost per lead is the total cost to generate a lead. For instance, if you were emailing 10,000 email offers and it cost you $100 per 1,000 pieces mailed for printing, mail services and postage, your total mail promotion cost would be

$1,000. If 300 responses were received, that would be a 3% response rate. By dividing $1,000 by 300 responses, you come up with your cost per lead. In this case, $3.00 is the cost for each lead received. But this is only half the equation for determining whether the promotion was successful.

You must determine what we call the back-end response, or your cost per order. If 30 people buy the product, this represents a 10% conversion-to-sales ratio from your generated leads. We know the promotion cost was $1,000. So, we divide $1,000 by 30 customers to get our cost per order, or $33 in this case. Consider all these factors as you evaluate your direct marketing program.

14

SHOULD YOU HAVE A CUSTOMER LOYALTY PROGRAM?

In 1981, American Airlines began a program that was to forever change the way business views and keeps its customers. The Advantage program was created to capture market share through a reward system for increased use of the airline for travel. Every airline in the industry quickly followed suit.

We call these Customer Loyalty Programs. And every business should evaluate whether such a program should be incorporated into their marketing program. There are a number of considerations before you jump into your own program. A Customer Loyalty Program is a long-term marketing strategy to create brand loyalty and is based on the 80/20 rule—80 percent of one's business comes from 20 percent of your customer base. A loyalty program rewards those who are willing to remain a loyal customer.

The digital age has made customer loyalty programs easier to manage and easier to target their customers through email.

Such programs do not have to be expensive and sophisticated. It may be as simple as a record store validation of five purchases to earn a sixth free purchase, or a credit card company awarding prizes based on the use of the card over a twelve month period. However, there are some important criteria to consider before you launch your own loyalty program. And not all businesses are ideal for such programs. They are most effective when the following criteria are met:

1. The product should be purchased on a frequent basis, allowing the customer to work toward a level of reward.

2. A product should have significant margin to enable you to support the program.

3. If you have competition in the market and customers are easily swayed from one product to another.

4. If you are able to support the program with database systems, personnel, capital and follow through.

5. Your company should be driven to providing service to your customers. If you are not, this program is not for your company.

6. A long-term commitment. If not, the program will backfire and you'll be worse off than you were before you began such a program, due to disgruntled customers.

One important piece of information you should know is whether your customers buy your products or services exclusively or do they buy from your competitors also. If you determine that they don't buy from your competitors, you're simply adding unneeded cost to your marketing program. However, if they are, you have the opportunity to generate more incremental sales and brand loyalty from those customers and gain market share from your competition.

CHAPTER

15

THE ROLE OF SOCIAL MEDIA, ONLINE AND EMAIL MARKETING

A lot has changed in the advertising landscape since I owned an ad agency in the 1980s and 1990s. The Internet has changed the way marketing and advertising is done today. Target marketing and relationship building has become the DNA of marketing today. Estimates are that Facebook social network reaches 1.6 billion monthly active users as of this writing. The ability to target user preferences is scary! It has become the marketers dream tool to target an individual.

Google has the same capability to target user preferences making online marketing one of the most cost effective means of reaching an audience. However, it is not always a straight transactional strategy that can be employed. It is often indirect in how an effective sales process is employed.

Social media is a hybrid element of the promotion mix because in a traditional sense it enables companies to talk to their customers, while in a nontraditional sense it enables customers to talk directly to one another. A 2014 survey of 2800 marketers found 97% are using social media.

Using social media to market a product or service requires patience and investment of time creating an online community. The goal of using Facebook to market a product or service involves building a community of friends who are willing to engage with you. Getting them to click the Like button in order to create engagement around your messaging is the goal in social media marketing.

Most marketers get frustrated with Facebook if they expect a direct return immediately. Social media guru Sandi Krakowski explains that you must be posting at least 8-10 times a day and only 20% of any post can be offer related. Otherwise, your friends will simply perceive that you are trying to sell them and not really interested in having a relationship. Personal interaction is key.

Twitter, the other major player in social media is another key relationship strategy tool for marketers today. It has become a fine-tuned science with very few understanding and keeping up with the changes that occur in this space to make it profitable for the average company. All social media is designed to build relationships between people and their various networks. Those who understand how to effectively use these tools are able to profit from these new mediums of marketing.

Salesforce's Pardot, a website that features research on marketing and advertising using email and social media cites that "Email marketing, while still a prominent marketing tool, is most effective today as a nurturing platform than for acquiring leads. Pardot conducted an online survey in June of 2012 to determine the role of email in Business-to-Business marketing strategies. The survey covered topics ranging from email marketing best practices to usage and testing, and was completed by more than 100 anonymous Business-to-Business marketers in the United States.

Usage Trends

A majority of Business-to-Business companies (65%) allocate less than 25% of their budgets to email marketing, while only 9% are devoting more than 50% of their budgets to email efforts. The survey also indicated that 70% of Business-to-Business marketers do not consider email marketing to be a primary lead generation tactic. 'Instead of using email, most marketers are using a variety of other lead generation tactics to get that initial prospect information into their systems,' explains Adam Blitzer, co-founder and COO of Pardot. 'Email marketing is then used to move new leads through the sales process or to re-engage dormant leads.'

Yet email still has a major role in marketing campaigns:

- More than 60% of Business-to-Business marketers are using email for drip nurturing.

- Of those, 65% are using targeted messaging, by changing which emails are sent based on how a prospect responds.

'The fact that email is being used more for drip nurturing than lead generation isn't that surprising,' said Blitzer. 'We're moving into an age that places more emphasis on communicating through various channels. While companies are still using email, they're also using landing pages, forms, social media, paid search ads, and more to generate leads.'"

LinkedIn

LinkedIn is the largest professional social network for business to business marketing online today with an astounding 135 million users and a targeted audience of business professionals. If you are in business and you do not have a presence on LinkedIn, you are missing valuable opportunities to connect and grow your business.

Leveraging the power of LinkedIn begins with building a solid professional profile and presence. As a professional, how do you stand out from the crowd on LinkedIn? How do you differentiate yourself from the millions of professional users on the network? What will make your profile visitors want to learn more about you and your business to ultimately connect with you? You must first establish a foundation in order to begin building your influence, generating introductions and referrals, and uncovering valuable business opportunities. LinkedIn suggests that having a completed profile provides you with a 40% greater chance for networking success, and they make it easy for you to understand how to achieve that 100% completion. Having a completed profile is the most effective way to showcase all of who you are through your talents, background, experience, passions, interests, and areas of expertise. In addition, a completed profile is going to make you appear to be a more competent user in the network.

Your LinkedIn profile may be the first stop for a new introduction. With a solid foundation, you will be well positioned for the next phase, where you can grow your influence and build your business.

There is a lot more you need to know about LinkedIn that can be found in a great ebook which I have provided a link to below. Check out all the strategies in this ebook to help you develop an ongoing strategy on LinkedIn.

Want to learn more about LinkedIn? Check out this free ebook: http://cdn2.hubspot.net/hub/53/blog/docs/ebooks/learning_linkedin_from_the_experts.pdf

16

INFORMATION MARKETING

"The Big 3 Mega-Niches"

David Ogilvy, founder of one of the largest ad agencies in the world said: "A blind pig can sometimes find a truffle. But it helps to know that they're found in oak forests."

Eben Pagan, a very successful information marketer says, "As it turns out, most of the money that's made in Information Products, Advice, Consulting and Coaching is made within a few key 'Mega-Niches.' If you know what these are, it can give you a huge head start over everyone else - and get you far down the path of targeting your money-making Information Product niche (or your next product)."

These three Mega-Niches are:

1. Health & Fitness

2. Dating & Relationships

3. Business & Money

If you look at all of the "big hits" in Information Products, probably 80%-90% of them are within one of these categories. If you're targeting a niche, and you're looking for a need you can fill with your product or service, then START HERE.

There are patterns that successful information marketers follow. They invest a great deal into the relationship before they ask you to invest money. Information marketing is a science. Consequently, you will find successful information marketers will give you something that has perceived value on the front end. It could be an ebook, a series of podcasts, or videos. They will provide a tangible benefit to you. This is designed to do a few things: 1) build relationship, 2) build trust, 3) demonstrate knowledge about the product or service.

A friend of mine who was very successful in the real estate information marketing business says it is important to make sure you communicate simply around a particular product or service and not give customers too many options. He says, "A confused mind does not buy." For instance, limit the number of products you try to sell. Focus your attention on the core product you are selling and limit their options.

A few years ago we launched a series called 3greatestlies.com. This is a teaching series designed to expose Satan's lies that he speaks to people. Our program consists of an opening 2 minute video that invites you to view 3 20 minute videos you receive 48 hours apart. There is a reason to give some time between the videos in order to create a desire for the program. All of the videos are free and they deliver a very valuable teaching that has helped thousands of people. At the conclusion of our third video we give you an option to purchase our 20-part Change Agent video course and you are enrolled in our Change Agent Network for the five months it takes to go through our course. One course is sent one time a week for 20 weeks. The course costs $47 a month.

Do you have a product or service you want to sell? Consider the information marketing approach.

17

BUILDING A BUSINESS
BY BLOGGING

I never could have imagined that when I started writing TGIF Today God Is First daily email blog it would someday be read by a quarter of a million people daily in over 100 countries. I also would never have imagined my income would be derived from those who support our ministry because of receiving our blog. God has a sense of humor to take a guy who barely got out of English class and make him a writer of fifteen books. The ways of God are surely not our ways.

If I can do this, you can do this.

Are you passionate about something? Do you have a product or service you can write about? Are you knowledgeable about a topic others might find interesting? If so, you might be a candidate to start your own blog. The internet has made the playing field equal for all writers. You have access to the same world everyone else has access to. Your job is to create something others will find interesting or valuable.

Here are some key things to know why blogs can help you market a product or service.

- It allows you to demonstrate your knowledge and expertise on a subject – you become an authority.

- It helps drive traffic to your website.

- It helps convert that traffic into leads.

- It drives long-term results that can result in transactions or sales.

Each day our TGIF devotional goes out to several hundred thousand people a day via email as well as being seen on Facebook and various other websites. Each of our blogs have links to products and services that we offer through Marketplace Leaders. We have our own in-house bookstore that has a website that directs people there from our blog. We promote our events and products through our blog. We also allow people to support our ministry through tax-deductible gifts. This has allowed us to support a ministry for the last twenty years.

Check us out at *www.TodayGodIsFirst.com*

CHAPTER

18

SMART PHONES:
THE NEW MARKETING WAVE

The major trend of the future is for people to make buying decisions and conduct research via their smart phone.

A research report in 2014 found that the global smartphone market has witnessed extraordinary growth in recent years, with shipments rising by 40 percent in 2013 to exceed the 1 billion unit threshold and $266 billion in value. A 2013 study found that 46% of users relied exclusively on mobile devices in their pre-purchase research with 55% of mobile retail shoppers making a purchase.

The report says that most smartphone shoppers convert in stores, while tablet shopping tends to be completed online (56 percent). The report says that 77% of smartphone-based purchase activity occurs in-person, offline.

Conclusion: Make your product info available using a smartphone. Most websites must be optimized for mobile application.

Repurposing Your Content

Once you begin to create content you will want to repurpose your content. What that means is you make your content available in other forms.

Mobile Apps are another tool that marketers must use to build relationships and sell their product or service. We decided to use mobile apps to repurpose our TGIF devotional content. We have two apps, one that is exclusively designed to deliver the TGIF devotional content. There is a one-time cost of $2.99 to purchase this app for iPhone or Android. iPhone and Android keep 1/3 of the revenue and the publisher gets to keep 2/3 of the fee.

The other app we call our TGIF Multi-media App. This app is designed to build relationships with our audience. We provide podcasts, videos, our speaking calendar and you can even make purchases from our bookstore on the app. Currently our TGIF Multi-media app costs $120 a month for hosting. Our TGIF app does not cost us any hosting fees. We believe our apps help us serve our customer and contribute to building relationships with our core audience. We do not necessarily see these as directly producing income but certainly contributes to serving our clients who support us with their donations.

There is usually a one-time production fee to make your app. Some programs involve a monthly hosting fee combined with an initial production fee.

To download our apps please visit:
http://www.marketplaceleaders.org/apps/

19

STEPS TO GREAT SALES LETTERS

There is a science to writing a good sales letter. In this chapter I want to share some proven principles from great direct marketing writers. Today we live in a soundbyte culture. Fewer and fewer people read full-length books. However, it would be wrong to assume all your sales letters must be short.

Direct marketers have learned that length of copy has nothing to do with response. Long copy sells better if done well. If you are making a purchase of a very expensive product, you are going to want to know everything you can about that product. That requires more information. The key is making the information interesting and compelling. Take a look at some of these examples: www.stopyourdivorce.com, (generates $15-20k a month after 10 years of offering a $79 ebook!). www.doubleyourdating.com, ($20 million a year) Both sites generate tens of thousands of dollars each month.

Sometimes too low of a price makes a prospect think it is no good. As mentioned earlier, there are 37 factors to the sales process.

1. Great headline – must be one primary, strong benefit in the headline

2. Strong sub-head benefit or promise to support it.

3. Remind the reader of their pain. Identify with their struggle. Sympa-

thize with them.

4. Tell your personal story. Let the reader identify with you and that you can relate to their pain. Tell them why you are qualified to speak to them about this topic.

5. "It's not your fault." Explain why they may be in the pain they are in and sympathize with it and ask rhetorical questions.

6. Content. Try me. i.e., Apple lets you put your hands on the product. Free trial.

7. Incorporate free content in letter, free video, etc.

8. Credibility. Why me? Give them value in the letter by including information in the letter

9. Explain the product and what is in it. How does it work, features and benefits – the service itself.

10. Bullet points follow of the benefits and features.

11. Who needs and who does not need it? i.e. "If you are not going through adversity right now, chances are you really don't need this product (Upside book), but if you are in adversity, this book was written for you."

12. What makes this product different than other products on the market or other programs?

13. Wrap up. Repeat what you will get. Price and details on how to order.

14. Money back guarantee. i.e. 30 day money back guarantee

Your Close – Your Signature

15. PS. Repeat headline promise

16. Testimonials. Can drop in throughout copy but must be toward end of letter, not in the beginning.

17. Get feedback to your letter. Give them a place to let you tell you about what you have said.

18. Give free downloads before they ever commit.

ADDITIONAL RESOURCES
BY OS HILLMAN

Visit *www.MarketplaceLeaders.org* or *www.TGIFBookstore.com*

Receive TGIF Today God Is First and to stay connected to Os Hillman:

iPhone - TGIF iPhone App & Podcast through iTunes.com
www. marketplaceleaders.org/apps/

Email – *www.TodayGodIsFirst.com*

Facebook – *www.facebook.com/pages/TGIF-Today-God-Is-First*
Website – *www.TodayGodIsFirst.com*

Follow Os:

Twitter - *@oshillman*

LinkedIn – *Os Hillman*

Marketplace Community – *www.MLcommunity.com*

Change Agent Network – *www.BecomeaChangeAgent.net*

Other Books by Os Hillman

For additional resources from Os Hillman visit *www.tgifbookstore.com*

Listening to the Father's Heart devotional

Change Agent: How to be the one who makes a difference

Experiencing the Father's Love: How to live as sons and daughters of our Heavenly Father

The 9 To 5 Window: How Faith Can Transform The Workplace.

The Upside of Adversity: From the Pit to Greatness

TGIF Today God Is First, Volume 1 & 2

Making Godly Decisions

The Purposes of Money

Are You a Biblical Worker? Self-assessment

The Faith@Work Movement: What every pastor and church leader should know

TGIF Small Group Bible Study– Faith & Work: Do They Mix?

Proven Strategies for Business Success

Visit Our Websites

www.MarketplaceLeaders.org

www.Reclaim7Mountains.com

www.tgifbookstore.com

www.UpsideofAdversity.com

www.mlcommunity.com

www.becomeachangeagent.com

www.3GreatestLies.com

Marketplace Leaders
PO Box 69
Cumming, GA 30028
678.455.6262
info@marketplaceleaders.org
www.marketplaceleaders.org

ABOUT
THE AUTHOR

Os Hillman owned and operated an ad agency from 1984 to 1996. During this time he served clients such as American Express, Steinway Pianos & Sons, US Kids Golf, Peachtree Software, ADP Payroll Services, S&S Mills Carpet, Parisian Department stores and many non-profit organizations.

Today Os Hillman is president of Marketplace Leaders and Aslan Group Publishing and is involved in several entrepreneur ventures related to publishing and internet marketing. He is an author, speaker, consultant and recognized authority in the role that faith and ethics play in the marketplace. He is author of fifteen books and a daily internet email blog entitled TGIF Today God Is First that is read by several hundreds of thousands of people daily in 104 countries.

Os attended the University of South Carolina on a golf scholarship and was a golf professional for three years before going into business in 1980. He resides in Cumming, Georgia, a northern suburb of Atlanta.

www.ingramcontent.com/pod-product-compliance
Lightning Source LLC
Chambersburg PA
CBHW050522210326
41520CB00012B/2405